4096469

D0143566

THE GREAT PHILOSOPHERS

Consulting Editors
Ray Monk and Frederic Raphael

WITTGENSTEIN

P. M. S. Hacker

ROUTLEDGE
New York

Published in 1999 by
Routledge
29 West 35th Street
New York, NY 10001

First published in 1997 by
Phoenix
A Division of the Orion Publishing Group Ltd.
Orion House
5 Upper Saint Martin's Lane
London WC2H 9EA

10 9 8 7 6 5 4 3 2 1

Library of Congress Cataloging-in-Publication Data

Hacker, P. M. S. (Peter Michael Stephan)
        Wittgenstein / P. M. S. Hacker.
          p. cm.—(The great philosophers : 1)
        Includes bibliographical references.
        ISBN 0-415-92376-X (pbk.)
        1. Wittgenstein., Ludwig, 1889–1951. I. Title. II.
        Series: Great Philosophers (Routledge (Firm)) : 1.
B3376.W564H244 1999
192—dc21   99-14479
                                                          CIP

WITTGENSTEIN

on Human Nature

INTRODUCTION

Ludwig Wittgenstein was born in Vienna in 1889. He came to Britain to study aeronautical engineering at Manchester University in 1908. A growing interest in the foundations of mathematics and logic took him to Cambridge in 1911 to work with Bertrand Russell. There he began work on what was to become his first great masterpiece. With the outbreak of war, he returned home to enlist in the army. Despite his involvement in heavy fighting on the Russian and Italian fronts, by 1918 he had completed his book: the *Tractatus Logico-philosophicus*, which was published in 1921. Its primary themes were the general nature of representation, the limits of thought and language, and the character of logical necessity and of the propositions of logic. Its greatest achievement was its elucidation of the truths of logic, not as the most general laws of thought (as they were commonly conceived to be) or as the most general truths about the universe (as Russell held), but rather as tautologies which are true come what may and say nothing at all, but which constitute forms of proof. The book was the primary inspiration for the Vienna Circle, the fountainhead of the movement known as 'logical positivism' which flourished in the inter-war years. It was also the major influence on the Cambridge school of analysis in the 1920s and 1930s. The *Tractatus* engendered the 'linguistic turn' characteristic of twentieth-century analytic philosophy, directing philosophical investigation and methodology towards the study of the logic of our language and its use.

After completing the *Tractatus*, Wittgenstein abandoned the philosophy for a decade. In 1929 he returned to

3

Cambridge and resumed work. The first years were spent dismantling the philosophy of the *Tractatus*, in which he now saw grave flaws, and replacing it with a diametrically opposed viewpoint. Over the next sixteen years he worked on what was to become his second, posthumous masterpiece: the *Philosophical Investigations* (1953). In it he presented a revolutionary conception of philosophy, a completely new approach to the philosophy of language and a highly original philosophy of mind. Side by side with this, he worked extensively on the philosophy of mathematics, in which his results were no less radical than in the other parts of philosophy on which he wrote. Although he published nothing, through his teaching and his pupils he exerted great influence upon the development of analytical philosophy in Britain in the post-war years. After his death in 1951, the flood of his posthumous books ensured that his thought dominated Anglophone philosophy for the next quarter of a century.

Wittgenstein's philosophical psychology undermined the Cartesian, empiricist and behaviourist traditions. In place of the Cartesian *res cogitans* – a spiritual substance which is the bearer of psychological properties, Wittgenstein put the human being – a psychophysical unity, not an embodied *anima* – a living creature in the stream of life. For it is human beings, not minds, who perceive and think, have desires and act, feel joy and sorrow. By contrast with the Cartesian and empiricist conception of the mental as an inner realm of subjective experience contingently connected with bodily behaviour, Wittgenstein conceived of the mental as *essentially manifest* in the forms of human behaviour which give *expression* to 'the inner'. While the Cartesians and empiricists alike thought of the inner as 'private' and truly known only to its introspecting subject, Wittgenstein denied that introspection is a faculty of 'inner sense' or a source of knowledge of private experience at all.

On the other hand, he insisted that others could often know perfectly well about what is thus 'private' to oneself. While Cartesians and behaviourists represented behaviour as bare bodily movement, Wittgenstein emphasized that human behaviour is, and is experienced as being, suffused with meaning, thought, passion and will.

The very conception of the nature of a human being that had dominated the philosophical tradition was distorted. It had been distorted not through folly or blindness, but by the pressure of philosophical questions concerning the essence of the self, the nature of the mind, the possibility of self-knowledge, the relation of mind and body, and the possibility of knowledge of other minds. It was in the struggle to answer such questions, which seemed to *demand* certain kinds of answer, that the Cartesians and empiricists subtly and progressively twisted our concepts of person, human being, mind, thought, body, behaviour, action and will out of all recognition. Hence it is these puzzles that must first be solved or *dissolved* before we can hope to attain a correct human point of view and to see ourselves aright.

In this book, I shall sketch some of Wittgenstein's reflections on these great themes. It will be fruitful to do so against a backcloth of his radical conception of philosophy, for the movement on centre-stage will be highlighted by the setting.

WITTGENSTEIN'S CONCEPTION OF PHILOSOPHY

Throughout its history, philosophy has always been thought to be part of the general quest for truth. The physical sciences aim at knowledge of the laws of nature; the a priori mathematical sciences were conceived to give us knowledge of the laws of number and space. Since philosophy was likewise thought to aim at knowledge, it too must have a subject matter of its own. This was variously conceived. According to Platonists, the aim of philosophy is the investigation of abstract objects – Platonic Ideas or Forms – which will disclose the essential natures of all things. Aristotelians thought of philosophy as continuous with the sciences, distinct from the special sciences primarily in its generality. Its role is to investigate the fundamental principles of each science and of reasoning in general. Cartesians held philosophy to be foundational. Its task is to lay the foundations of all knowledge on secure and indubitable grounds. The British empiricists, by contrast, thought of philosophy as an investigation into the origins of our ideas, the extent and nature of human knowledge. The Kantian revolution shifted ground: the task of philosophy is to uncover the preconditions for the *possibility* of knowledge in any given domain, the upshot of which should be an array of propositions which are both necessary truths about the realm of experience and nevertheless known independently of experience. Common to this long tradition was the conviction that philosophy is a cognitive discipline: that is, that it aims at truth, and strives to add to human knowledge.

Despite two and a half millenniums of endeavour, there is no agreed canon of philosophical knowledge. There are no well-established philosophical laws or theories on the model of the empirical sciences, nor are there proven philosophical theorems on the model of the a priori theorems of mathematics. It is tempting to explain this fact by reference to the intrinsic difficulty of the subject, but to argue that philosophy is now on the brink of delivering its long-awaited results. Such promises ring hollow, for they have been made with tiresome regularity over many centuries by successive philosophers. The failure of philosophy to establish a body of certified knowledge needs a more convincing explanation.

It was characteristic of Wittgenstein not to take sides in pre-existing philosophical debates, weighing up the pros and cons of the arguments and siding with the most persuasive. Rather, he strove to uncover the points of agreement between the disputing parties, the shared presuppositions which were taken for granted by all, and to challenge these. 'One keeps forgetting to go right down to the foundations,' he wrote. 'One doesn't put the question marks *deep* enough down' (CV 62). In the debate about the nature of philosophy, he questioned the assumption that philosophy is a cognitive discipline in which new knowledge is discovered, theories are constructed, and progress is marked by the growth of knowledge and well-confirmed theory. He wrote ironically:

> I read 'Philosophers are no nearer to the meaning of "Reality" than Plato got ...' What an extraordinary thing. How remarkable that Plato could get so far! Or that we have not been able to get any further. Was it because Plato was *so* clever? ...
>
> You always hear people say that philosophy makes no progress and that the same philosophical problems which were already preoccupying the Greeks are still troubling us today. But people who say that do not understand the reason why it has to be so. The reason is that our language has remained the same and always introduces us to the same questions. As long as there is a verb 'to be' which seems to work like 'to eat' and 'to drink'; as long as there are adjectives like 'identical', 'true', 'false', 'possible'; as long as people speak of the passage of time and of the extent of space, and so on; as long as all this happens people will always run up against

> the same teasing difficulties and will stare at something
> which no explanation seems able to remove. (BT 424)

Philosophical problems arise primarily out of misleading features of our language, for our language presents very different concepts in similar guise. The verb 'to exist' looks no different from such verbs as 'to eat' or 'to drink', but while it makes sense to ask how many people in College don't eat meat or drink wine, it makes no sense to ask how many people in College don't exist. To be red is a property some things have and other things lack, but is existence a property some things have and others lack? Things may come into existence and later cease to be – but does that mean that they acquire a property they initially lacked and later lose it? It makes sense to investigate the nature of various things that exist, but it makes little sense to investigate the nature of existence or 'Being', let alone of non-existence or 'Nothing' (as Heidegger tried to). In philosophy we are constantly misled by grammatical similarities which mask profound logical differences. So we ask questions which are intelligible when asked of certain categories of things, but which make no sense or a very different sense when asked of things that belong to a different category. Philosophical questions are frequently not so much questions in search of an answer as questions in search of a sense. 'Philosophy is a struggle against the bewitchment of our understanding by means of language' (PI §109).

Philosophy is categorically different from science. Science constructs theories, which enable us to predict and explain events. They are testable in experience, and may only approximate the truth. But in this sense of 'theory', there can be none in philosophy. The task of philosophy is to resolve or dissolve philosophical problems by clarification of what makes sense. But any determination of sense antecedes experience, and is presupposed by true or false judgements. There can be nothing hypothetical in philosophy, for it cannot be a *hypothesis* that a proposition one understands makes sense. In the sense in which science explains phenomena – that is, by causal hypotheses and hypothetico-deductive inference from a statement of laws and initial conditions – there are no explanations in philosophy. The only kinds of explanation in philosophy are explanations by *description* – description of the use of words. This Wittgenstein does, *inter alia*, by describing 'language-games': the practices, activities, actions and reactions in characteristic contexts in which the rule-governed use of a word is integrated. These descriptions and associated explanations of meaning are not a philosophy, but a methodology. According to Wittgenstein what is distinctively philosophical is the purpose which they serve. Describing the use of words is a method for disentangling conceptual confusions – confusions that arise, *inter alia*, through the unnoticed misuse of words. It serves to resolve or dissolve philosophical problems. An approximation to sense, unlike an approximation to truth such as occurs in science, is one form or another of nonsense. In so far as philosophical difficulties are produced by our unwitting abuse of our existing concepts, they cannot be resolved by replacing these with different concepts, since all that does is to sweep the difficulties under the carpet. It is the business of philosophy not to resolve a contradiction or paradox by means of a conceptual innovation, but rather to attain a clear view of the conceptual structure that troubles us: the state of affairs *before* the contradiction is resolved. We get entangled in the rules for the use of our expressions, and the task of philosophy is to get a clear view of this entanglement, not to mask it. There can be no discoveries in philosophy, for everything that is relevant to a philosophical problem lies open to view in our rule-governed use of words. All the information we need lies in our knowledge of how to use the words we use, and of this we need only to be reminded. 'The work of the philosopher consists in assembling reminders for a particular purpose' (PI §127): namely, for the purpose of resolving philosophical, conceptual, problems.

Philosophy has a double aspect. Negatively, it is a cure for the diseases of the intellect. Philosophical problems are symptoms of conceptual entanglement in the web of language. Success lies in disentangling the knots, making the problem disappear, just as success in treating a disease lies in making it disappear and restoring the patient to good health. In this respect,

> Philosophy results in the disclosing of one or another piece of plain nonsense and in the bumps that the understanding has got by running its head up against the limits of language. These bumps make us see the value of that disclosure. (PI §119)

To be sure, this negative aspect may well seem destructive,

> since it seems to destroy everything interesting, that is, all that is great and important.[1] (As it were all the buildings, leaving behind only bits of stone and rubble.) What we are destroying is nothing but houses of cards and we are clearing up the ground of language on which they stand. (PI §118)

More positively, philosophy is a quest for a perspicuous representation of segments of our language which are a source of conceptual confusion. Our grammar, the rules for the use of our words (syntax *and* lexicon), is lacking in surveyability – it cannot be taken in at a glance. And some segments of language – psychological terms such as 'mind', 'thought', 'experience', etc. – present greater barriers to attaining an overview than others, such as terms in

10

engineering. For the surface grammar of expressions – that part that can be taken in at a glance, such as the distinctions between nouns, verbs and adjectives – is often misleading. The verb 'to mean' in sentences such as 'I meant him' looks as if it describes an act, but it does not; the substantive 'the mind' looks as if it is the name of a substance or thing, like 'the brain', but it is not; the possessive 'have' in the sentence 'I have a pain' looks as if it signifies possession, as in the sentence 'I have a penny', but it does not. Hence 'The concept of a perspicuous representation is of fundamental significance for us. It earmarks our form of representation, the way we look at things' (PI §122). A perspicuous representation provides us with a map of the conceptual terrain.

> The aim is a surveyable comparative representation of all the applications, illustrations, conceptions [of the relevant part of the grammar of a philosophically problematic array of expressions] ... The complete survey of everything that may produce unclarity. And this survey must extend over a wide domain, for the roots of our ideas reach a long way. (Z §273)

Such an overview produces just that understanding which consists in seeing conceptual connections which we commonly overlook, and which, if overlooked, generate confusion. A perspicuous representation is a rearrangement of the rules for the use of words which lie open to view, with which we are indeed perfectly familiar, but which are not readily taken in as a whole. They *become surveyable* by such a rearrangement which makes clear the *logical* character of the words that baffle us in philosophical reflection. Hence, 'The problems are solved, not by giving new information, but by arranging what we have always known' (PI §109).

This may appear to trivialize a profound subject, reducing philosophy to a matter of mere words. But this is deceptive.

There is nothing trivial about language. We are *essentially* language-using creatures. Our language, and the forms of our language, mould our nature, inform our thought, and infuse our lives.

> The problems arising through a misinterpretation of the forms of our language have the character of *depth*. They are deep disquietudes; their roots are as deep in us as the forms of our language and their significance is as great as the importance of our language. (PI §111)

This may appear to render philosophy easy – merely a matter of clarifying the use of words, so that the solution of its problems is readily obtained. But this too is mistaken:

> How is it that philosophy is such a complicated structure? After all, it should be completely simple if it is that ultimate thing, independent of all experience, that it claims to be. – Philosophy unravels the knots in our thinking; hence its results must be simple, but its activity is as complicated as the knots it unravels …
>
> Why are grammatical problems so tough and seemingly ineradicable? – Because they are connected with the oldest thought habits, i.e. with the oldest images that are engraved into our language itself. (BT 423)

Nowhere are the ancient images more pervasive, powerful and misleading than in our discourse about the mental. We speak of ideas being *in* the mind, as if the mind were a kind of space; of *introspecting* what is in the mind, as if introspection were a kind of seeing; of *having* a mind and a body, as if mind and body were kinds of possession; of having mental images 'before the mind's eye', as if mental images were non-physical pictures which a mental organ of sight can inspect; and so on. This ancient verbal iconography is not *false* – we do have ideas in mind, thoughts do flash across our minds, we often engage in reflective

12

introspection, people do have minds of their own and to be sure they have a body. But it *is* a kind of iconography. And we are misled by the imagery embedded in our language, no less than someone from a primitive culture might be misled by the literal iconography of Love (as a putto) or Death (as an aged man with a scythe) in western art. We misconstrue the meanings of these well-worn phrases, and construct houses of cards in our reflections on the nature of the human mind. It is far from easy to dislodge these picturesque but misleading images.

> Teaching philosophy involves the same immense difficulty as instructions in geography would have if the pupil brought with him a mass of false and falsely simplified ideas about the course and connections of rivers and mountains.
>
> People are deeply embedded in philosophical, i.e. grammatical confusions. And to free them from these presupposes pulling them out of the immensely manifold connections they are caught up in. One must, so to speak, regroup their entire language …
>
> Language contains the same traps for everyone; the immense network of well-kept false paths. And thus we see one person after another walking the same paths and we know already where he will make a turn, where he will keep on going straight ahead without noticing the turn, etc., etc. Therefore wherever false paths branch off I should put up signs which help one get by the dangerous places. (BT 423)

Wittgenstein's radical conception of philosophy is exemplified in his treatment of the salient questions in the philosophy of mind – questions about the nature of the mental, about the 'inner' and the 'outer', about our knowledge of ourselves and of others. It is vindicated by the extent to which he sheds light upon what puzzles us, and thereby dissolves or resolves our problems.

MIND, BODY AND BEHAVIOUR: THE POWER OF A PHILOSOPHICAL ILLUSION

The thought that a human being is a composite creature consisting of body and soul (or mind, or spirit) is an ancient one. It is bound up with our fear of death, with the craving for an afterlife in a happier world, with our grief at the death of our loved ones and our longing to be reunited with them. It is associated with common phenomena of human lives which mystify us, such as dreaming, in which we seem to inhabit a different world, unconnected with our sleeping body, or in which we seem to have commerce with the dead. It is connected with more recherché phenomena, such as visionary experiences and 'out of the body' experiences. And it is deeply rooted in the grammar of our languages.

This conception, in different forms, was articulated in the religious and philosophical thought of antiquity and the Middle Ages. It was given its most powerful philosophical expression in our era by Descartes. According to Descartes, a human being is composed of two distinct substances, the mind and the body. A person's innermost self, that in which his essential identity consists, and that to which he refers when he uses the first-person pronoun 'I', is his mind or soul, the *res cogitans*. The essence of the mind is thought, the essence of the body extension. A person is an embodied anima, for while the body is destructible, the mind or soul is not. Interaction between the two is causal, being mediated by the pineal gland in the brain. In perception, stimulations of the nerve endings in the body affect the mind, giving it ideas of the environment. In volition, the will brings about motions of the limbs. What passes in one's own mind is immediately accessible to oneself by consciousness – one is invariably conscious of, and knows indubitably, what one is thinking, feeling or wanting. The minds of others are only indirectly knowable, by inference from what they do and say.

Cartesian dualism provided the agenda for philosophers for the next three centuries. They found much to disagree with. The idea of an immaterial soul-substance was found wanting. If the mind is immaterial and non-spatial, what would differentiate two or two dozen minds all enjoying the same experiences? In other words, what is the principle of individuation for immaterial substances? Even if experiences require a substance in which to inhere (since experiences must surely be the experiences *of something*), the persistence of the same substance seems, as Locke argued, irrelevant to the self-identity of a person through time, for that requires only psychological, mnemonic, continuity. Moreover, what grounds in experience do we have for supposing there to be any soul-*substance* constituting the self at all? As Hume famously remarked, 'when I enter most intimately into what I call *myself*, I always stumble on some particular perception or other, of heat or cold, light or shade, love or hatred, pain or pleasure. I never can catch *myself* at any time without a perception, and never observe anything but the perception.'[2] The self or *Ego*, that immaterial thing to which Descartes thought the first-person pronoun refers, is not itself an object of experience. Is it not a mere fiction? Had Descartes not confused the unity of one's own subjective experience with the experience of a unity – of a soul-substance or ego, as Kant argued? And how can an immaterial, non-spatial substance interact causally with a physical body in space? Is it not absurd to suppose that all statements about voluntary human action, such as

15

promising, paying a bill, speaking or writing, are analysable into descriptions of mental acts of volition and of consequent bodily movements?

The Cartesian myth, like all great myths, is insidious. It can assume many guises, and even those who think of themselves as liberated from Cartesianism adopt crucial elements of the tale. A striking feature of contemporary philosophers, psychologists and neurophysiologists is that, while rejecting mind/body dualism, they accept the fundamental conceptual structure of the Cartesian picture. While rejecting the idea of an immaterial substance, they are prone to *identify* the mind with the brain (sometimes speaking of 'the mind/brain'), or the mental with the neural – arguing that mental states just *are* states of the brain. Alternatively, it is argued that the mind stands to the brain as the software of a computer stands to its hardware – that the brain is, as it were, a biological computer, and man a machine. There is no difficulty in envisaging causal interaction between the brain and the body; hence Descartes' difficulties regarding interaction are apparently readily resolved. The brain is conceived to be an information-processing device. The afferent nerves from the sense organs transmit information to the brain, which the brain processes to yield perception. Perceiving something is thought to be identical with a brain state produced by the informational input. Wanting and believing are conceived to be identical with brain states which are the cause of the bodily movements that we make when we act voluntarily. Consciousness is compared with a self-scanning mechanism in the brain; hence the knowledge which we allegedly have of our current experience is explained by reference to consciousness thus conceived. In short, mind/body dualism has been replaced by brain/body dualism, immaterial substance by grey glutinous matter, and the large part of the general structure of the Cartesian picture survives intact.

Wittgenstein was little concerned with the details of the philosophical systems of his predecessors. His preoccupation was with the roots of philosophical error, in particular with its *grammatical* roots – and by 'grammar' he meant not merely syntax, but *all* the rules for the use of words, including those that fix their meaning. Hence I shall first sketch a composite picture of the philosophical conception of human beings which he was concerned to expose as illusion. It is, at first blush, a natural and tempting picture. But we should be forewarned – what is most natural in philosophy is to err. And

> What we 'are tempted to say' in such a case, is, of course, not philosophy – but its raw material. Thus, for example, what a mathematician is inclined to say about the objectivity and reality of mathematical facts, is not a philosophy of mathematics, but something for philosophical *treatment*. (PI §254)

We speak of the 'external world' of physical objects, states, events and processes in space. But, as Frege put it, 'even an unphilosophical man soon finds it necessary to recognize an inner world distinct from the outer world, a world of sense impressions, of creatures of his imagination, of sensations, of feelings and moods, a world of inclinations, wishes and decisions'.[3] The physical world is public, accessible to all by perception. The mental world is the world of subjective experience. It too consists of objects (pains, mental images, sense-impressions), states (of joy or sorrow), events (the occurrence of a thought, a pain, a sudden recollection) and processes (thinking, calculating) – although these are mental and mysterious, curiously aethereal, intangible. To have an experience, such as a pain, is to stand in a relation to such a mental object. The

17

proposition 'A has a penny' describes a situation in the physical world, whereas the proposition 'A has a pain' describes a situation in the inner world. One can *have* a penny, and one can *have* an idea – possess a coin or possess a thought. While objects in the physical world may be owned or ownerless, objects in the inner world must be owned by a subject. 'It seems absurd to us that a pain, a mood, a wish should go around the world without an owner independently. A sensation is impossible without a sentient being. The inner world presupposes someone whose inner world it is.'[4] Moreover, the items in the inner world are *essentially private*: 'Nobody else has my pain. Someone may have sympathy with me, but still my pain belongs to me and his sympathy to him. He has not got my pain, and I have not got his feeling of sympathy.'[5] I cannot have the same pain as you, but only a similar one. Experiences are inalienable 'private property'.

When the owner of an inner realm has an experience, he cannot doubt it. I cannot have a pain and doubt or wonder whether I do, cannot think I have a pain and be wrong. I *know indubitably* that I do – and if someone were to challenge me, I should reply, 'Surely I must know whether I have a pain or not.' In short, 'we find certainty in the inner world, while doubt never leaves us in our excursions into the external world'.[6] What perception is for the external world, introspection, consciousness or awareness is to the inner world. What the subject observes introspectively he reports for others in such sentences as 'I have a pain', 'I want such and such', 'I intend to do so and so', which *describe* how things are with him. Such descriptions of private, subjective experience are given independently of one's behaviour – I do not look to see whether I am groaning before I can report that I have a pain, nor do I wait to see what I say before I know what I think. So the 'inner' –

18

the subjective – is epistemically independent of the 'outer' – of bodily behaviour.

Clearly, one cannot know of the inner world of others as one knows one's own. One can introspect only one's own mind. Rather, one observes the behaviour of others, and infers from this what experiences are causally responsible for their behaviour. The mental states of others are *hidden*, inaccessible to direct observation by outsiders. Even if they tell us how things are with them, what is given in such communication is merely words, and, to be sure, these may be lies. However another behaves, it may always be dissimulation. The behaviour of others is the outer husk behind which lies private experience. The body that behaves is just a physical organism, subject to the causal laws that govern all physical bodies. Behaviour is mere physical movement and emission of sounds. Since a person may have an experience or be in a certain mental state without showing it, and since pretence is possible, the connection between behaviour and the mental is non-logical. Hence the inference from the behaviour of others (e.g. their cries when they injure themselves) to their mental states or experiences (e.g. their being in pain) cannot be logical. But it cannot be inductive either, since inductive correlation presupposes non-inductive identification, and I cannot directly identify, be acquainted with, the experiences of others. So the inference must be by analogy with my own case: when I am injured, I have a pain and cry out; I observe others injuring themselves and then crying out, and infer that they too feel pain. Alternatively, it must be a hypothetical inference to the best explanation: that is, from the observation of certain effects to the existence of unperceived entities which are hypothesized as their causes) on the model of scientific inferences to unobserv-ables: that is, the best explanation of the behaviour of others is that it is caused by hidden and unobservable experiences. So one cannot have genuine *knowledge* of the inner life of others, as one does of one's own. One can at best *surmise* or *believe* that things are thus-and-so with them.

This picture of human nature is widely held. It is, Wittgenstein argued, misguided in every respect, even though it contains kernels of truth 'seen through a glass darkly'. For it is indeed based on features of our language, but it distorts and misrepresents them. His criticisms demolish the Cartesian picture and undermine contemporary brain/body dualism equally effectively.

PRIVATE OWNERSHIP OF EXPERIENCE

The temptation to conceive of experiences as privately owned and inalienable is great. 'If we are angry with someone for going out on a cold day with a cold in his head, we sometimes say: "I won't feel your cold". And this can mean: "I won't suffer when you catch a cold". This is a proposition taught by experience' (BB 54). But we also 'say "I *cannot* feel your toothache"; when we say this, do we only mean that so far we have never as a matter of fact felt someone else's toothache? Isn't it rather, that it's logically impossible?' (PR 90). But there is a confusion lurking here:

> For we could imagine a, so to speak, wireless connection between the two bodies which made the one person feel pain in his head when the other had exposed his to the cold air. One might in this case argue that the pains are mine because they are felt in my head; but suppose I and someone else had a part of our body in common, say a hand. Imagine the nerves and tendons of my arm

and A's connected to this hand by an operation. Now imagine the hand stung by a wasp. Both of us cry, contort our faces, give the same description of the pain, etc. Now are we to say we have the same pain or different ones? If in such a case you say: 'We feel pain in the same place, in the same body, our descriptions tally, but still my pains can't be his', I suppose as a reason you will be inclined to say: 'because my pain is my pain and his pain is his pain'. And here you are making a grammatical statement about the use of such a phrase as 'the same pain'. You say that you don't wish to apply the phrase, 'he has got my pain' or 'we both have the same pain', and instead, perhaps you will apply such a phrase as 'his pain is exactly like mine'. (BB 54)

But this is confused on three counts. First,

If the word 'toothache' means the same in 'I have toothache' and 'He has toothache', what does it then mean to say he can't have the same toothache as I do? How are toothaches to be distinguished from one another? By intensity and similar characteristics, and by location. But suppose these are the same in both cases? But if it is objected that the distinction is simply that in the one case *I* have it, in the other *he*; then the owner is a defining mark of the toothache itself. (PR 90)

But the 'owner' of pain is not a property of the pain. Rather, *having a pain* is a property of the suffering person. Two distinct substances are distinguishable by the different properties they severally have, but the pain I have is not differentiated from the pain you have by belonging to me rather than to you. That would be like arguing that two books cannot have the same colour, since *this* red colour belongs to *this* book and *that* red colour belongs to *that* book.

21

Second, this amounts to claiming that two people cannot have the numerically same pain, but only a qualitatively identical one. But 'Consider what makes it possible in the case of physical objects to speak of "two exactly the same", for example, to say "This chair is not one you saw here yesterday, but is exactly the same as it"' (PI §253). The distinction between numerical and qualitative identity is a distinction which applies to physical objects, space-occupying particulars, but not to *qualities* – or to pains. If two people both have a sharp throbbing pain in their left eye, then they have the same pain – neither qualitatively *nor* numerically the same, just the same – and may well be suffering from the same disease.

Third, to have a pain is not to own anything. One might object:

> States or experiences, one might say, owe their identity as particulars to the identity of the person whose states or experiences they are. From this it follows immediately that if they can be identified as particular states or experiences at all, they must be possessed or ascribable … in such a way that it is logically impossible that a particular state or experience in fact possessed by someone should have been possessed by anyone else. The requirements of identity rule out logical transferability of ownership.[7]

To such an objection Wittgenstein replies: '"Another person can't have my pains." – *My* pains, what are they supposed to be? What counts as a criterion of identity here?' (PI §253). In other words, the phrase '*my* pains' does not specify *what* pains I have, does *not* identify my pains at all. It merely specifies *whose* pains I am speaking of. The criteria of identity of pain – that is, the criteria by which we determine *what* pain we are speaking of – are given by specifying its intensity, phenomenal characteristics and location (a dull, throbbing pain in the left temple). But the question 'What pain?' is distinct from the question 'Whose pain?' Two people can and often do have the same pain. To *have* a pain is no more to own anything, logically or otherwise, than is to have a bus to catch. *My* pain is not the pain that *belongs* to me, but simply the pain I have – but to say that I have a pain is not to say *what* pain I have. It is misleading to conceive of pains as particulars. To have a pain (or a mental image, or an idea) is not to own a kind of mental *object*. Though we speak of things (although not pains) as being *in* the mind, the mind is not an inner stage and what is in the mind is not a protagonist in a private play.

The first-person pronoun 'I', *pace* Descartes, does not refer to my mind (that I have a toothache does not mean that my mind has a toothache). One reason why we are deluded here is that, when we say such things as 'I háve a pain',

> we don't use ['I'] because we recognize a particular person by his bodily characteristics; and this creates the illusion that we use this word to refer to something bodiless, which, however, has its seat in our body. In fact *this* seems to be the real ego, the one of which it was said, 'Cogito, ergo sum'. – 'Is there then no mind but only a body?' Answer: The word 'mind' has meaning, i.e. it has a use in our language; but saying this doesn't yet say what kind of use we make of it. (BB 69f.)

'I' no more refers to an immaterial entity than do 'you', 'he' and 'she'. Nor does it refer to the body: 'I am thinking' does not mean that my body is thinking. Is the mind then just an aspect of the body? 'No', Wittgenstein replied, 'I am not that hard up for categories' (RPP II §690). Build, height and weight are aspects of the body. To have a mind of one's own is to be independent in thought, decision and action.

To make up one's mind is to decide, and to be in two minds whether to do something is to be undecided. To have an idea cross one's mind is suddenly to think of something; to have an idea at the back of one's mind is to have an incipient thought; to keep something in mind is not to forget it; to call something to mind is to recollect it; something out of mind is forgotten or not thought about: and so on.

EPISTEMIC PRIVACY

We construe the mind as an inner world to which only it's 'owner' has access. If only the 'owner' can *have* a given experience, then it seems plausible to hold that only he can know what experience he has – for someone else *logically* cannot have the same experience, and cannot 'peer into the mind' of another person. But private ownership of experience is an illusion. Epistemic privacy is also illusory, but more than one prop holds it in place, and each misleading support needs to be removed.

We are inclined to think that we have privileged access to our own mind by introspection. 'The word introspection need hardly be defined – it means, of course, the looking into one's own mind and reporting what we there discover. Everyone agrees that we there discover states of consciousness.'[8] Surely we are *aware* of our inner states, are *conscious* of them. This faculty of 'inner sense' is the source of our knowledge of the inner. That knowledge seems *certain* and *indubitable*: 'when a man is conscious of pain, he is certain of its existence; when he is conscious that he doubts or believes, he is certain of the existence of these operations'.[9] Indeed, some philosophers have held the mind to be *transparent* to the subject, and the deliverances of consciousness to be incorrigible. Hume argued that

> Since all actions and sensations of the mind are known to us by consciousness, they must necessarily appear in every particular what they are, and be what they appear. Everything that enters the mind, being in reality a perception, 'tis impossible anything should to *feeling* appear different. This were to suppose that even where we are most intimately conscious, we might be mistaken.[10]

Others disagreed, holding error to be possible, but they did not doubt that knowledge of the inner is obtained by inner sense. Their point was rather that 'introspection is difficult and fallible; and that difficulty is simply that of all observation of whatever kind'.[11]

Our talk of introspection is metaphorical. I may see that another sees something, but not that I do; hear what he is listening to, but not perceive that I am hearing something. I can no more *look into* my mind than I can look into the mind of another. There is such a thing as introspection, but it is not a form of inner perception. Rather, it is a form of self-reflection in which one engages when trying to determine, for example, the nature of one's feelings (e.g. whether one loves someone); it is 'the calling up of memories; of imagined possible situations, and of the feelings that one would have if ...' (PI §587). Such soul-searching requires imagination and judgement, but no 'inner eye', for there is nothing to *perceive* – only to reflect on.

When one has a pain or thought, sees or hears, believes or remembers something, one can *say so*. But the ability to say so does not rest on observing objects, states or events in one's mind. There is no such thing as an inner sense, there are no inner conditions of observation which might be poor or optimal (no 'More light!' or 'Louder please!'), nor can one move closer to any observed mental 'object' and have another look. There is such a thing as observing the course of one's pains or the fluctuation of one's emotions, but this is a matter of registering how one feels, not of *perceptually* observing anything. One may be conscious or aware of a pain, but there is no difference between having a pain and being conscious or aware of it – one cannot say, 'He is in severe pain, but fortunately he is not aware of it' or 'I have a pain, but since I am not conscious of it, it is really quite pleasant'. To be aware or conscious of a pain, of a mood, or of thinking does not belong to the category of *perceptual* awareness. Of course, unlike other sentient creatures, we can *say* that we have pain when we do. But we must not confuse the ability to say how things are with us with the ability to *see* (with the 'mind's eye', by introspection) – and thence think that *that* is why we can say what is 'within' us. To be able to say that one has a headache, that one believes such-and-such, that one intends to do so-and-so, is not to have access, let alone privileged access, to anything perceptible, for one does not *perceive* one's headache, belief or intention.

Nevertheless, do we not *know* how things are with us? Can I be in pain and *not* know it? And when I thus know that I am in pain, am I not *certain*? Can I be in pain and nevertheless *doubt* or *wonder* whether I am? Wittgenstein's response was dramatic and original: 'It can't be said of me at all (except perhaps as a joke) that I *know* that I am in pain. What is it supposed to mean – except perhaps that I *am* in pain?' (PI §246).

> 'I know what I want, wish, believe, feel …' (and so on through all the psychological verbs) is either philosophers' nonsense, or at any rate not a judgement *a priori*.

'I know ...' may mean 'I do not doubt ...' but does not mean that the words 'I doubt ...' are *senseless*, that doubt is logically excluded.

One says 'I know' where one can also say 'I believe' or 'I suspect'; where one can find out. (PI p. 221)

I can know what someone else is thinking, not what I am thinking.

It is correct to say 'I know what you are thinking', and wrong to say 'I know what I am thinking'.

(A whole cloud of philosophy condensed into a drop of grammar.) (PI p. 222)

The compression is excessive and Wittgenstein's drop of grammar must be evaporated if we are to see the cloud of philosophy it condenses.

In repudiating the idea of privileged, direct access to our own mental states, Wittgenstein was not affirming the idea that we have unprivileged, indirect access. In denying that we always *know* what mental states we are in, he was not claiming that we are sometimes *ignorant* that we are, for example, in pain. He did not reject the putative certainty of the inner in order to affirm its dubitability. Rather, he rejected the received picture not because it is *false* and its negation true, but because it and its negation alike are nonsense or, at least, do not mean what philosophical reflection takes them to mean. He turns our attention to our use of words, to what he called 'grammatical rules', with which we are familiar, in order to show how we go wrong. We mistakenly construe a grammatical connection or exclusion of words for an empirical or metaphysical connection or exclusion determining the essential nature of the mind.

Seeing and hearing are ways of acquiring information about our surroundings. Having a toothache, feeling depressed and expecting something are not ways of acquiring knowledge about our pains, moods and expectations. It makes sense to say that a person knows that *p* only if it also makes sense to deny that he does – for an ascription of knowledge is supposed to be an empirical proposition which is informative in so far as it *excludes* an alternative. But we have no use for the form of words 'I was in terrible pain but I didn't know this' or 'He was in agony but he didn't know it'. If 'A was in pain but didn't know it' is excluded, then so too is 'A was in pain and knew it'. 'I know I am in pain' can be a claim to *know* something only if 'I do not know whether I am in pain' is intelligible. But there is no such thing as being ignorant of whether one is in pain – if A said, 'Perhaps I am in agony, but I don't know whether I am', we would not understand him. There is room for indeterminacy (is it just an ache or a pain?) and for indecision ('I am not sure what I think about that'), but not for ignorance. It makes sense to talk of knowing where it also makes sense to talk of finding out, coming to know, or learning. But when one has a pain, one does not *find out* that one has. One does not come to know or learn of one's pains, one *has* them. If one knows that *p*, one can answer the question 'How do you know?' by adducing evidence or citing a perceptual faculty used in the acquisition of the knowledge. But one cannot say, 'I know that I have a pain because I feel it', for to feel a pain (unlike to feel a pin) just *is* to have a pain; and the question 'How do you know that you are in pain?' has no sense. Where we speak of knowing that *p*, we can also speak of guessing, surmising and conjecturing that *p*. But it makes no sense to guess that one is in pain. In short, our conception of epistemic privacy of experience confuses the *grammatical* exclusion of ignorance (the *senselessness* of 'Perhaps I am in pain, but I don't know whether I am', the fact that we have given *no use* to this form of words) with the presence of knowledge.

One might think that there is nevertheless a difference between being in pain and knowing that one is. For one must be conscious of the pain, be aware of it, which is something only *self-conscious* creatures can do. But to be aware of or conscious of a pain just is to have a pain – this is a distinction without a difference. It is striking that we do not say of our sick pets that they know that they are in pain – or that they do not know. When our cat is suffering, we do not console ourselves with the thought that, although the poor thing is in pain, luckily it does not know it because it is not a self-conscious creature. Animals do not *say* that they are in pain, whereas human beings do. That they do not say so does not show that they are ignorant, and the fact that we do does not show that we are better informed. It shows that we have learnt to manifest pain in ways unavailable to animals who cannot speak. A self-conscious being is not a creature who is conscious of his aches and pains, but rather one who is aware of his motives, knows what moves him and why, who reflects on his emotions and attitudes. That, indeed, is a capacity which only language-users have, and here error, doubt and self-deception are possible. Such self-knowledge, genuine self-knowledge, is hard won – it is not given by any supposed transparency of the mental. Others often know us better than we do ourselves.

Indeed, the very idea of the transparency of the mental is confused. It is intelligible to say that something is as it appears only if it also makes sense to say that it is other than it appears. But 'It seems to me that I have a pain, although in fact I don't' and 'You think you are in pain, but actually you are not' are senseless. So one cannot go along with Hume in arguing that it is a distinctive feature of the mental that things are exactly as they appear and that therefore we know how things are in our private inner world. Similar confusion of grammatical exclusion with empirical absence characterizes the thought that subjective experience is indubitable or even incorrigible. To be sure, I cannot doubt whether I am in pain, but not because I am certain that I am. Rather, nothing counts as doubting whether one is in pain. Doubt is not refuted by available grounds for certainty, but excluded by grammar. It is senseless to say, 'I may be in pain, but I am not sure'. 'I thought I was in pain, but I was mistaken' is nonsense. Reid was right to say 'I cannot be deceived by consciousness' with regard to my sensations, but not because I am so perceptive or because consciousness is so reliable – rather because *there is no such thing as deception* in this domain (although, of course, there is such a thing as self-deception in the domain of feelings and beliefs – which is another tale). 'I cannot make a mistake here' is not like 'I cannot make a mistake in counting from 1 to 10', but like 'I cannot be beaten at solitaire'.

Does this mean that there is no use for the form of words 'I know that I have ...' in the domain of the mental? No – only that they do not have an *epistemic* use.

> If you bring up against me the case of people's saying 'But I must know if I am in pain!', 'Only you can know what you feel', and similar things, you should consider the occasion and purpose of these phrases. 'War is war' is not an example of the law of identity either. (PI p. 221)

'I know I am in pain' may be just an emphatic assertion that one is in pain; or it may be an exasperated concession ('I am indeed in pain, you needn't keep on reminding me'). And 'Surely I must know if I am in pain' can be used to emphasize the exclusion of ignorance and doubt, and so as a way of specifying a grammatical rule – that it makes no *sense* not to know or to doubt that one is in pain. Wittgenstein was not legislating about usage, but describing it. He was pointing out that certain forms of words do not have the use they appear to have and cannot be used to support the philosophical theories which invoke them.

> If I say 'This statement has no sense', I could just point out statements with which we are inclined to mix it up, and point out the difference. This is all that is meant. – If I say 'It seems to convey something and doesn't', this comes to 'it seems to be of this kind and isn't'. This statement is senseless only if you try to compare it with what you can't compare it with. What is wrong is to overlook the difference. (LSD 359)

I can say how things are with me, and typically *my word* has privileged *status*. This is not because I have access to a private peep-show and describe what I see in it, which others cannot see. Rather, what I say is an *expression* of the inner. 'I have toothache' is often an *expression* of pain, comparable to a moan. 'I want to win' is not a *description* of my state of mind but a *manifestation* of it. 'I think (or believe) such-and-such' is an *expression* of opinion. This must be clarified.

DESCRIPTIONS AND EXPRESSIONS

Perception is a primary source of knowledge of the world. We perceive the facts, as it were, and read off their description from what we perceive, depicting what we thus apprehend in words. If we think of the inner as a private world to which the subject has privileged access, then we will be prone to think that here too we read off a description, such as 'I have a pain', 'I believe he is out' and 'I intend to go', from the facts accessible to us alone. Other features encourage this misguided thought. (1) Propositions such as 'A is angry' describe a person, characterizing his mental state. But if 'A is angry (wants X, intends to V)' is a description, then so too surely is 'I am angry (want X, intend to V)'. For does not the first-person utterance say of the speaker precisely what the corresponding third-person statement says of him? Indeed, is not the first-person utterance grounds for the third-person one precisely because it describes how things are with the speaker and *therefore* provides the evidence for the third-person description? (2) Not only is there this apparent logical symmetry between first- and third-person sentences, there seems a further tense symmetry. 'I had toothache yesterday' describes how things were with me. But does it not say of me precisely what 'I have toothache' said yesterday of me? (3) A true proposition describes things as they are. The assertion that A has toothache is true if and only if A has toothache. But A's utterance 'I have toothache' may be true (if he is sincere) or false (if he is lying). It is true if and only if he has toothache. So one and the same fact makes the two assertions true. So surely, they express the very same proposition, describe the same state of affairs and are true in virtue of what they thus describe.

These apparent logical symmetries generate the very epistemological picture that we have now begun to challenge. If 'I have a pain' is no less a description than 'He has a pain', then it seems it is one that is *justified* by the facts. So I am justified in asserting it only in so far as I know it to be true. But to know it to be true, I must verify it – by introspection, by comparing it with the facts to which only I have direct access. And if introspection is the method of verification of first-person present-tense statements about the inner, then third-person statements cannot be directly verified at all, but must be analogical inferences, or inferences to the best explanation. We have gone wrong somewhere. But, as Wittgenstein remarked, 'To smell a rat is ever so much easier than to trap it' (MS 165 152).

A fundamental reorientation of our thought is necessary. We must 'make a radical break with the idea that language always functions in one way, always serves the same purpose: to convey thoughts – which may be about houses, pains, good and evil, or anything you please' (PI §304), 'As if the purpose of the proposition were to convey to one person how it is with another: only, so to speak, in his thinking part and not in his stomach' (PI §317). For on the *cognitivist* account, the function of 'I have a pain' or 'I intend to V', etc. is to convey something I *know* to others, something which I apprehend by introspection and then describe in words for the benefit of others.

> We are so much accustomed to communication through speech, in conversation, that it looks to us as if the whole point of communication lay in this: someone else grasps the sense of my words – which is something mental: he as it were takes it into his own mind. If he then does something further with it as well, that is no part of the immediate purpose of language.
>
> One would like to say 'Telling brings it about that he *knows* that I am in pain; it produces this mental phenomenon; everything else is inessential to the tell-ing.' As for what this queer phenomenon of knowledge is – there is time enough for that. Mental processes just are queer. (It is as if one said: 'The clock shows us the time. *What* time is, is not yet settled. And as for what one tells the time *for* – that doesn't come in here.') (PI §363)

We must get away from the preconception that the fundamental role of the first-person psychological utter-ance is to *describe* how things are with us, to impart a piece of privileged information to others. When the child hurts himself and screams, he is not imparting to his mother a piece of information which he has attained by introspection, and the response 'How interesting' is out of place. Rather, the child manifests pain and his mother consoles him. And when the adult groans, 'I have a terrible pain', he is not conveying an item of knowledge to his hearer. If one is asked, 'Where is N.N.?' and one replies, 'I belive he is in London', the response 'What an interesting piece of autobiography; now tell me where N.N. is' would be a joke. If one says to the bar-tender, 'I want a scotch', he does not reply, 'Really; what else have you to tell me?' These utterances are *expressions* of pain, belief and desire respectively, not *descriptions* of objects and events on a private stage.

We must beware of too facile a use of the word 'description': 'Perhaps the word "describe" tricks us here. I say "I describe my state of mind" and "I describe my room". You need to call to mind the differences between the language-games' (PI §290). The concepts and activities that belong with describing one's room are observing, scrutinizing, examining, descrying. Here questions of perceptual competence (good or poor eyesight) and observational conditions (day or dusk) can be raised. The upshot may be identifying or misidentifying, recognizing or failing to recognize what is visible. One may be trained to observe better, and there are more or less skilful observers. One may make mistakes and correct them on closer inspection. It makes sense here to ask, 'How do you know?' or 'Why do you think so?', for in many cases one has evidence for one's identifications and characterizations. One may be certain (and yet wrong) or unsure of one's description. Not so in the case of many typical first-person present-tense psychological utterances such as 'I have a pain', 'I intend to be there', 'I believe he is in London', 'I am so pleased' and 'I'm afraid'. Used spontaneously in appropriate circumstances, they diverge markedly from the above paradigm of description (and from other members of the family, which we shall not examine). First, they are not grounded in perception. Hence, second, there are no observational conditions, no organs of perception, no perceptual faculty of 'inner sense', and no skills in apprehending one's pains, fears, intentions or beliefs. Third, one does not recognize or fail to recognize, identify or misidentify how things are with one (although there is room for realization, for example, that one's pain is a symptom of angina pectoris or that one's intentions are disreputable). 'I thought I had a pain but I was wrong' makes no sense. Fourth, there is no such thing as checking what one has said by looking more closely (but only, in certain cases, by reflecting further), no comparison of what one has (a pain, a thought, an emotion) with paradigms for correctness or accuracy of description. Fifth, as noted, there is here no knowledge or ignorance, certainty or doubt, but only indecision ('I'm not sure what I'll do' does not mean that I intend something but have to find out what it is; rather it means that I haven't yet made up my mind). Finally, one's utterance does not rest on evidence, and it makes no sense to ask, for example, 'How do you know that you are in pain?' or 'Why do you believe that you intend to go?'

None of this implies that there is no such thing as describing one's state of mind; but it is a rather more specialized language-game than one might think. It is something at which a highly self-conscious person, such as a Proust, excels. Whether a use of a form of words counts as a description of a state of mind depends upon the context and manner of utterance, upon the antecedent discourse, the tone of the speaker and his purposes. The concept of a state of mind is more restrictive than one assumes. Intending, believing and thinking are not states of mind, and to say what one intends, believes or thinks is never to describe one's state of mind. States of mind are states of consciousness (e.g. moods, emotional states) which have genuine duration: that is, they lapse during sleep and can be interrupted and later resumed. They are typically described in the imperfect or progressive tense, interwoven with descriptions of one's actions and reactions. And such spontaneous utterances as 'I'm going', 'I think he's in London' and 'I don't believe you' are not such descriptions. The classical picture nevertheless exerts a compelling force:

> There seems to be a *description* of my behaviour, and also, in the same sense, a description of my pain! The one, so to speak, the description of an external, the other of an internal fact. This corresponds to the idea that in the sense in which I can give a part of my body a name, I can give a name to a private experience (only indirectly).
>
> And I am drawing your attention to this: that the language-games are very much more different than you think.
>
> You couldn't call moaning a description! But this shows you how far the proposition 'I have toothache' is from a description ...
>
> In 'I have toothache' the expression of pain is brought to the same form as a description 'I have five shillings'. (LPE 262f.)

In place of the descriptivist, cognitivist, conception, Wittgenstein proposes a completely different picture – an *expressivist*, *naturalist* one. The verbal expression of pain is grafted on to the *natural* expressive behaviour in circumstances of injury, for 'The origin and the primitive form of the language-game is a reaction; only from this can the more complicated forms develop. Language – I want to say – is a refinement, "in the beginning was the deed"' (CV 31).[12]

How do words *refer* to sensations? – There doesn't seem to be a problem here; don't we talk about sensations every day, and name them? But how is the connection between the name and the thing named set up? This question is the same as: how does a human being learn the meaning of the names of sensations? – of the word 'pain' for example? Here is one possibility: words are connected with the primitive, the natural, expressions of the sensation and used in their place. A child has hurt himself and he cries; and then adults talk to him and teach him exclamations and, later, sentences. They teach the child new pain-behaviour.

'So are you saying that the word "pain" really means crying?' – On the contrary: the verbal expression of pain replaces crying and does not describe it. (PI §244)

A child cries out when he injures himself, grimaces, screams or groans, and assuages the injured limb. Here lie the roots of the language-game, not in observations of a private peep-show. There is no room here for asking the child how he knows that he has hurt himself, and we do not ask him whether he is sure that it hurts – we comfort him.

Something similar holds of other psychological terms – though not for all, and not for the more developed forms of psychological states and conditions. A child who wants his teddy reaches for it and cries out in frustration – we teach him the use of 'I want'. In reaching for his teddy, he does not first introspectively identify his inner state as volitional, and he no more does so when he says, 'I want Teddy.' A child is frightened by a barking dog, he blanches with fear and shrinks back; he does not recognize his feeling as fear before he responds to the dog, and no more does he do so when he has learnt to say 'I am frightened'. A child shrieks with delight at a Christmas present; later he learns to exclaim 'Oh, I like that' – his primitive behaviour is no description, and nor is his later exclamation. These primitive forms of natural behaviour are antecedent to our learnt language-games. They provide the behavioural bedrock for them, the stock upon which verbal *manifestations* and *expressions* of the mental are grafted.

Avowals of pain are learnt *extensions* of natural expressive behaviour, and are themselves forms of behaviour. Rudimentary expressions of wanting are partial *replacements* of natural conative behaviour. Spontaneous expressions of emotion, 'I like ...', 'I love ...', 'I hate ...', are *manifestations* of affective attitudes. And like the natural forms of behaviour which these learnt utterances replace, such verbal forms of behaviour are *logical criteria* for corresponding third-person ascriptions of sensation, desire and emotion. It is not an empirical discovery based on inductive correlation that human beings cry out, moan, assuage their injury when they hurt themselves, try to get what they want, or fear what they take to be dangerous. There is no such thing as a non-inductive identification of pain in one's own case, which can then be inductively correlated with pain-behaviour. 'We must not look for "toothache" as something independent of behaviour. We cannot say: "Here is toothache, and here is behaviour – and we can put them together in any way we please"' (LSD 298). For in one's own case, one does not *identify* one's toothache, one *manifests* it. It is part of what we mean by 'toothache' that it is exhibited in these forms of pain-behaviour. We learn to say, 'He is in pain' when he behaves thus, and his utterance 'It hurts' is no less a criterion for being in pain than the groan. Of course, pretence and dissimulation are sometimes possible (though not with the neonate – for pretence too has to be learnt); and the criteria for being in pain do not *entail* that the person is in pain. They are logically good evidence, which is, in certain circumstances, *defeasible*. But if not defeated, the criteria confer certainty.

Not all the psychological terms are thus connected with natural manifestations of the inner. There is such a thing as primitive intending behaviour: 'Look at a cat when it stalks a bird; or a beast when it wants to escape' (PI §647). But 'I'm going to V' or 'I intend' are not partial substitutes for this behaviour as an avowal of pain is a partial substitute for a groan. Rather, we are taught that when one says, 'I'm going to V', one must then go to V – but one is not taught first to identify an inner state of intending, which one then describes with the words 'I intend'. Dreaming is different again. The child wakes up screaming, 'Mummy, a tiger is chasing me' and its mother replies, 'No dear, you had a dream – look, you are in your own room and there is no tiger here'; gradually the child will learn to say, 'I dreamt ...' on awaking. 'I think ...' and 'I believe ...' are not learnt or used to describe an inner state which we observe within ourselves and then describe for the benefit of others. Rather, they are used to qualify a claim about how things are – to signify that we are not in a position to guarantee the sequel (that we are not in a position to vouch for it or to claim knowledge of it), to signify that we are unsure or that, even if sure, we acknowledge that doubting is not irrational. The pegs upon which different psychological terms hang are various, but the differences do not reinstate the classical picture of the inner.

THE INNER AND THE OUTER: KNOWLEDGE OF OTHERS

The complement of the misconception of privileged access is that we can know how things are with others only indirectly, that the 'inner' is *hidden* behind the 'outer' (i.e. mere behavioural externalities – bodily movements and the sounds of speech). This too, Wittgenstein argued, is a misconception – but not because the inner is, as the behaviourists argued, a fiction. Far from it: pleasure and pain, joy and grief are not mere behaviour. But contrary to the Cartesian and empiricist traditions, mental objects, events, states and processes are not just like physical ones save for being immaterial; and *pace* Hume, the mind is *not* 'a kind of theatre, where several perceptions successively make their appearance; pass, re-pass, glide away, and mingle in an infinite variety of postures and situations'.[13] It is such a *philosophical conception* of the inner that is a *grammatical fiction* which Wittgenstein aimed to extirpate. The inner is much more *unlike* the outer than such philosophical construals of it suggest.

Our talk of 'inner' and 'outer' is metaphorical. One does not normally say that toothache is something 'inner' or that pain is 'mental'. On the contrary, we speak of *physical* pain and contrast it with mental suffering such as grief. Toothache is in teeth, not in the mind (although it is not in a tooth in the sense in which a cavity is). But we compare toothache and its expression with 'internal' and 'external', for I do not say I have toothache on the grounds of observation, but I say that he has toothache on the grounds of his behaviour. So 'We must get clear about how the metaphor of revealing (outside and inside) is actually applied by us; otherwise we shall be tempted to look for an inside behind that which in our metaphor is the inside' (LPE 223). Someone may have toothache and not manifest it, may see and not say what he sees, may think and not voice his thoughts. But if he moans with toothache, describes what he sees, voices his opinion, then he has 'revealed' what is, in our metaphor, the inner. If he screams when the dentist prods his tooth, we cannot say, 'That is mere behaviour – his pain is still concealed.' If he tells us what he thinks, we cannot say, 'That is just words, but he keeps his thoughts to himself.' And if he shows us what he sees, then we too can see what he sees, without looking inside anything. For this is what is *called* 'manifesting pain', 'saying what one thinks', 'showing what one sees'. Barring insincerity, he does not leave anything behind which he keeps to himself. Insincerity and dissimulation are possible – what is 'outer' may deceive us with regard to what is 'inner' – but the evidence for such deception consists in further *behaviour*: that is, in more of the 'outer'.

One can conceal one's pain, hide one's feelings and keep one's thoughts secret. But to have a toothache, feel angry or think something is not to conceal anything. One hides one's pain when one deliberately suppresses one's groan – and one reveals it when a cry bursts from one's throat. One conceals one's feelings when one exercises self-restraint, and reveals them when one loses self-control and vents one's anger. One hides one's thoughts not by thinking them and not expressing them, but rather by keeping one's diary in code, or talking to one's wife in the presence of the children in a language they do not speak. But if the code is cracked and the diary read, or if the foreign language is understood, then one's thoughts are revealed.

It is similarly mistaken to claim that one knows only *indirectly* how things are with others, for it makes sense to talk of *indirect* only if it makes sense to talk of *direct* knowledge. But as we have seen, it is misleading to say that someone *knows* that, for example, he has toothache, or thinks this or that – for this is not a case of knowledge at all, let alone of direct knowledge. But to see another writhing and groaning after being injured *is* to know 'directly' that he is in pain – it is not an inference from the fact that he has a prescription for analgesics. Witnessing the suffering of another is not acquisition of indirect knowledge, and the sufferer does not have direct knowledge – what he has is *pain*, not knowledge. If a friend opens his heart to one, one cannot say, 'I have only indirect knowledge of his thoughts and feelings.' That would be in place if one learnt of his thoughts by hearsay, at second hand.

These misconceptions of inner and outer, concealed and revealed, direct and indirect, go hand in hand with a deep-rooted misconception of human behaviour, a misconception which characterizes both Cartesian dualism and contemporary brain/body dualism. For both conceive of behaviour as bare bodily movement caused by the inner, muscular contractions and movements of limbs and face consequent upon mental and neural events. From these externalities, we *infer* their hidden causes. We *interpret* what we see as the outward manifestation of inner events and states. But it is not like that.

> 'I see the child wants to touch the dog but doesn't dare.'
> How can I see that? – Is this description of what is seen
> on the same level as a description of moving shapes and
> colours? Is an interpretation in question? Well, remem-
> ber that you may also *mimic* a human being who would
> like to touch something, but doesn't dare. And what you
> mimic is after all a piece of behaviour. But you will also
> be able to give a *characteristic* imitation of this beha-
> viour only in a wider context ...
>
> But now am I to say that I really 'see' fearfulness in this
> behaviour – or that I really 'see' the facial expression?
> Why not? But that is not to deny the difference between
> the two concepts of what is perceived ... 'Similar
> expression' takes faces together in a quite different way
> from 'similar anatomy'. (RPP I §§1066–8)

The idea that we do not really see the joy, distress or humour in a person's face, but only muscular contractions, is as misguided as the idea that we do not really see the trees in the garden, but only patches of colour and shapes or only sense-data and appearances. A similar misconception attends the thought that what we hear when listening to another talking are mere sounds, which our brain then interprets as meaningful speech. Joy, distress or amusement are not hidden behind the face that manifests them, but visible on it. What we so misleadingly call 'the inner' *infuses* the outer. Indeed, we could not even describe the outer save in the rich terminology of the inner. We see friendliness or animosity in a face and do not infer its presence from the disposition of the facial muscles (which we could not even describe). Indeed, it is a mistake to think that we normally *infer* the inner from the outer:

> In addition to the so-called sadness of his facial features, do I also notice his sad state of mind? Or do I *deduce* it from his face? Do I say: 'His features and his behaviour were sad, so he too was probably sad'? (LW I §767)

One might infer that someone is in pain if one knows that he is suffering from arthritis. But when one observes someone writhing in agony, one does not infer that he is in pain from his movements – one sees that he is suffering. *Pain*-behaviour is a criterion of being in pain, as *joyous* behaviour is a criterion of being joyful. If it is objected that one can see *that* he is in pain, but one cannot see his pain – *that* one must infer – the reply is that (1) he cannot perceive his pain either, and (2) one cannot see his pain only in the sense in which one cannot see sounds or hear colours.

The thought that another person can only surmise that I am in pain (whereas I *know* I am) is wrong. 'If we are using the word "know" as it is normally used (and how else are we to use it?), then other people very often know when I am in pain' (PI §246). If a philosopher objects that, all the same, another cannot know with the certainty with which ` know, the reply is that 'I know', construed as the phil` sopher is construing it, is nonsense. True, another may doubt whether I am in pain, and I cannot – but then another may be certain that I am in pain, and I cannot. For, to be sure,

> I can be as *certain* of someone else's sensations as of any fact.
>
> 'But, if you are *certain*, isn't it that you are shutting your eyes in face of doubt?' – They are shut. (PI p. 224)

Why are they shut? Well, 'Just try – in a real case – to doubt someone else's fear or pain' (PI §303).

Can one say:

> 'I can only *believe* that someone else is in pain, but I *know* it if I am.' – Yes: one can make the decision to say 'I believe he is in pain' instead of 'He is in pain'. But that is all. – What looks like an explanation here, or like a statement about a mental process, is in truth an exchange of one expression for another which, while we are doing philosophy, seems the more appropriate one. (PI §303)

If it is not merely a decision to use this form of expression, then it is absurd to say that we can only attain *belief* regarding the states of mind of others:

> 'I believe he is suffering.' – Do I also *believe* that he isn't an automaton? ...
>
> (Or is it like this: I believe that he is suffering, but am certain that he is not an automaton? – Nonsense!) ...
>
> 'I believe he is not an automaton', just like that, so far makes no sense.
>
> My attitude towards him is an attitude towards a soul. I am not of the *opinion* that he has a soul ...
>
> The human body is the best picture of the human soul. (PI p. 178)

44

MINDS, BODIES AND BEHAVIOUR

Our psychological concepts are logically connected with the behaviour that manifests the inner. For it is the behaviour of a human being that constitutes the logical criteria for saying of him that he is perceiving or feeling something, thinking or recollecting, joyful or sad. Such behaviour is not bare bodily movements, but smiles and scowls, a tender or angry voice, gestures of love or contempt, and what a person says and does. Human behaviour is not a mere physical phenomenon like the appearance of a blip on a computer screen or the movements of an industrial robot.

This runs counter both to Cartesian dualism and to brain/body dualism. It is implicitly denied by our contemporaries who contend that computers can think (or will do so soon). Wittgenstein assails the presuppositions of such views:

> 'But doesn't what you say come to this: that there is no pain, for example, without *pain-behaviour*?' – It comes to this: only of a living human being and what resembles (behaves like) a living human being can one say: it has sensations; it sees; is blind; hears; is deaf; is conscious or unconscious. (PI §281)

Of course, one can be in pain and not show it, think and not say what one thinks. But

> one might say this: If one sees the behaviour of a living being, one sees its soul. – But do I also say in my own case that I am saying something to myself, because I am

behaving in such-and-such a way? – I do *not* say it from observation of my behaviour. But it only makes sense because I do behave in this way. (PI §357)

The subject of psychological predicates is a living creature who can and does manifest his feelings and thoughts in behaviour. A human being, a horse or a cat can be said to see or hear, be blind or deaf. But an electronic sensor neither sees nor is blind. A robot which responds to verbal instructions does not hear, and when it malfunctions it is not deaf. A computer does not become conscious when it is turned on, nor does it fall asleep when turned off.

What gives us *so much as the idea* that living beings, things, can feel?

Is it that my education has led me to it by drawing my attention to feelings in myself, and now I transfer the idea to objects outside myself? That I recognize that there is something there (in me) which I can call 'pain' without getting into conflict with the way other people use this word? – I do not transfer my idea to stones, plants, etc. (PI §282)

But it is not so. We do not learn the use of the word 'pain' by identifying a certain sensation within us, which we know occurs and which we recognize as such and then name. Rather, we learn to use the sentence 'I have a pain' as an extension of our natural pain-behaviour and to ascribe pain to others when they behave likewise. There is no such thing as identifying (or misidentifying), recognizing (or misrecognizing) our own pains, and the word 'pain' is given its meaning not by naming an inner object, but by being used in expressions of pain by the sufferer and by his cry 'I am in pain' being a criterion for others to ascribe pain to him.

It seems that sensations, perceptions, thoughts, indeed

consciousness itself, must be attributable either to physical things – human bodies or brains or computers – or to minds or souls, which some bodies have. Wittgenstein attacks this false dilemma with a subtle, indirect strategy:

> Couldn't I imagine having frightful pains and turning to stone while they lasted? Indeed, how do I know, if I shut my eyes, whether I have not turned into a stone? And if that has happened, in what sense will *the stone* have the pains? In what sense will they be ascribable to the stone? And why need the pain have a bearer here at all?!
>
> And can one say of the stone that it has a soul and *that* is what has the pain? What has a soul, or a pain, to do with a stone?
>
> Only of what behaves like a human being can one say that it *has* pains.
>
> For one has to say it of a body, or, if you like, of a soul which some body *has*. And how can a body *have* a soul?
> (PI §283)

Were we *per impossibile* to learn what 'pain' means by naming an inner object which we recognize, then ascribing pain to others would be problematic. One would have to imagine that some other thing *has* what one has oneself – namely *this* – in *his* body. But if *this* were in his body, that would simply mean that I felt a pain in *his body* rather than in mine.

> If one has to imagine someone else's pain on the model of one's own, this is none too easy a thing to do: for I have to imagine pain which I *do not feel* on the model of pain which I *do feel*. That is, what I have to do is not simply to make the transition in imagination from one place of pain to another. As, from pain in the hand to pain in the arm. For I am not to imagine that I feel pain in some region of his body. (Which would be possible.)

47

> Pain-behaviour can point to a painful place – but the
> suffering person is he who gives it expression. (PI §302)

If one can imagine another person's having a pain *on this
model*, can one not also imagine a stone's having a pain? If I
am to imagine a pain I do not feel on the model of a pain I
do feel, why should I not imagine a stone's having one too? If
I imagine turning to stone and my pain continuing,
would the stone have pain? But there is no such thing as a
stone manifesting pain. Why should the pain be the stone's
at all? One might just as well say that here there is a pain
without a bearer! But that is absurd. And it is equally absurd
to ascribe pain to a stone.

Do *I* then continue to have a pain after *my body* has
turned to stone? Is the bearer of pain then the soul or mind,
the Cartesian *res cogitans*, which belongs to the stone? So
the stone has a pain in as much as *its* mind has a pain! But
this is doubly absurd. First, the possessive form of representation for pain, as we have seen, does not signify
ownership; 'I have a pain' is an *expression of pain*, and the
expression of pain is *pain-behaviour* – but stones do not
behave. Nor, indeed, do minds or souls. Second, stones do
not have minds – it is living human beings, who laugh and
cry, act and react to the circumstances of their lives in
endless ways, who have minds. *I* have a body and a mind –
although the possessive 'have' is again misleading, since
'my body' does not signify a relationship of possession
between *me* and my body and 'I' does not refer to my body.
My body, however, does not *have* a mind. It is not the body
that exhibits pain in its behaviour, for it is not *bodies* that
behave – it is not my body that cries out and groans, grits its
teeth and behaves stoically. And if I turn to stone, the stone
does not have a soul or mind.

> Look at a stone and imagine it having sensations. – One
> says to oneself: How could one so much as get the idea

48

of ascribing a *sensation* to a *thing*? One might as well ascribe it to a number! – And now look at a wriggling fly and at once these difficulties vanish and pain seems to get a foothold here, where before everything was, so to speak, too smooth for it.

And so, too, a corpse seems to us quite inaccessible to pain. – Our attitude towards the living and towards the dead, is not the same. All our reactions are different. (PI §284)

We respond differently in innumerable ways to what is alive, and these natural reactions are not a consequence of a theory or a foundation for one, but constitutive of the human form of life and hence the bedrock of our language-games.

But isn't it absurd to say of a *body* that it has pain? – And why does one feel an absurdity in that? In what sense is it true that my hand does not feel pain, but I in my hand?

What sort of issue is: Is it the *body* that feels pain? How is it to be decided? What validates saying that it is *not* the body? – Well, something like this: if someone has a pain in his hand, then the hand does not say so … and one does not comfort the hand but the sufferer: one looks into his face.

How am I filled with pity *for this man*? How does it come out what the object of my pity is? (Pity, one may say, is a form of conviction that someone else is in pain.) (PI §§286f.)

Whether it is or is not the body that feels pain is not an empirical issue, but a logical or conceptual one. We do not say, 'This body feels pain.' We do not observe that this body must take an aspirin and go to the doctor, nor do we advise that this body should grin and bear it. Rather we speak c human beings as sufferers, not of their bodies or their minds. And the way we speak meshes with our lives, is interwoven with our behaviour, actions and reactions. We tend the injured limb, but we comfort the person who is injured and pity him. This sort of behaviour has pre-linguistic roots: 'a language-game is based *on it*, ... it is the prototype of a way of thinking and not the result of thought' (Z §541).

Wittgenstein's argument has direct bearing on contemporary neurophysiological psychology (and on brain/body dualism), for scientists are prone to ascribe to the brain those functions which the Cartesian tradition wrongly ascribed to the mind. For example,

> we can thus regard all seeing as a continual search for the answers to questions posed by the brain. The signals from the retina constitute 'messages' conveying these answers. The brain then uses this information to construct a suitable hypothesis about what there is ...[14]

> the brain gains its knowledge by a process analogous to the inductive reasoning of the classical scientific method. Neurons present arguments to the brain based on the specific features they detect, arguments on which the brain constructs its hypothesis of perception.[15]

But if psychological predicates make literal sense only if ascribed to the living animal or human being as a whole, and not to the body, then they can make no sense if ascribed to a part of the body: namely, the brain. One sees with one's eyes, not with one's mind or brain, and it is not one's mind or brain that sees, but rather the living human being. It is nonsense to ascribe toothache to one's mind or brain, for neither the mind nor the brain can *logically* manifest toothache in behaviour. The firing of neurons concurrently with pain is not a behavioural manifestation of the brain's being in pain, but a concomitant of the person's being in pain, and it is the person who manifests pain-behaviour, not his brain. And if it is nonsense to say 'my brain has toothache', it is 'nonsense on stilts' to claim that the brain poses questions and answers them, constructs hypotheses or understands arguments. These predicates make sense only as applied to human beings and creatures like us, and they are applied on the grounds of sophisticated linguistic behaviour. A brain cannot talk, not because it is dumb, but because it makes no sense to say, 'My brain is talking.' I may be a chatterbox, but my brain cannot. There is no such thing as a brain using a language. Brains do not have opinions, argue, hypothesize or conjecture. It is we who do so. To be sure, we could not do so if our brain were destroyed; but then we could not have toothache or walk without a brain either – yet it is not the brain that has toothache and walks to the dentist. If one is asked what one thinks of the weather, should one say, 'My brain is thinking it over; give it a minute, and it will tell me, and then I'll tell you'?

CAN MACHINES THINK?

Wittgenstein's arguments might seem to be refuted by the invention of computers, for do we not say that these machines compute and have powerful memories? Artificial-intelligence scientists say that their machines can recognize and identify objects, make choices and decisions, think. Chess-playing machines can beat chess-masters, and computers can calculate faster than mathematicians. Does this not show that the claim that such predicates are ascribable only to human beings and to what behaves like them has been overtaken by the march of science? Wittgenstein lived before the computer age. Nevertheless, he did reflect on these questions.

> 'Is it possible for a machine to think?' ... the trouble which is expressed in this question is not really that we don't yet know a machine which could do the job. The question is not analogous to that which someone might have asked a hundred years ago: 'Can a machine liquify gas?' The trouble is rather that the sentence, 'A machine thinks (perceives, wishes)' seems somehow nonsensical. It is as though we had asked 'Has the number 3 a colour?' (BB 47)

Today the question does *not* seem nonsensical – so accustomed have we become to our science-fiction and the jargon of computer scientists. But it is nonsense for all that. Wittgenstein approached the issue circuitously: 'Could a machine think? – Could it be in pain? – Well, is the human body to be called such a machine? It surely comes as close s possible to being such a machine' (PI §359). Science pularizers often write of the body as a 'biological machine', but even of such a 'machine' we do not say that it is in pain – for it is not my body that has a headache in its head, rather *I* do in *my* head.

> But a machine surely cannot think! – Is that an empirical statement? No. We only say of a human being and what is like one that it thinks. We also say it of dolls and no doubt of spirits too. Look at the word 'to think' as a tool.
> (PI §360)

The criteria for ascribing thought to a subject lie in behaviour in appropriate circumstances. But do computers not behave appropriately? Do they not behave, produce the desiderated results of calculation on their screens in response to the questions we ask them? Do we not say, as we wait for the answer to flash up, 'Now it's thinking'? Indeed – just as we say of our old car, 'She's getting temperamental.' Even if a computer were so programmed that the answers it displayed in response to the questions we typed into it were indistinguishable from the answers a human being might type (the 'Turing test'), the machine would not be behaving as a human being. It takes more, but not *additively* more, to answering a question than to make an appropriate noise or generate an inscription. The appearance of an appropriate inscription on the screen is a product of the behaviour of the programmer who designed the program, but not a form of human behaviour of the machine. The behavioural criteria in the stream of life for saying of a being that it is thinking can no more be exemplified by a computer than the number three can turn green with envy.

But does it not *calculate*? Not in the sense in which we do. The computer does not understand the results it types out, does not know what the symbols it displays mean, for it neither knows nor understands anything. It is all one to it whether it is linked to a screen which displays symbols or to a keyboard which plays notes. Does it not at any rate calculate mechanically? Only in the derivative, secondary sense in which a nineteenth-century calculating machine did. But in the sense in which *we* calculate, a being that can calculate mechanically can also calculate thoughtfully. If it can think, it can also reflect, ponder, reconsider (and there is no such thing as reconsidering mechanically). It must make sense to say of it that it is pensive, contemplative or rapt in thought. It must be capable of acting thoughtlessly as well as thoughtfully, of thinking before it acts as well as acting before it thinks. If it can think, it can have opinions, be opinionated, credulous or incredulous, open-minded or bigoted, have good or poor judgement, be hesitant, tentative or decisive, shrewd, prudent or rash and hasty in judgement. And this battery of capacities and dispositions must itself be embedded in a much wider skein. For these predicates in turn can be applied only to a creature who can manifest such capacities in behaviour, in speech, action and reaction in the circumstances of life. 'What a lot of things a man must do in order for us to say he *thinks*' (RPP I §563).

Intellectual capacities are not detachable from affective and conative ones, and these in turn cannot be severed from perceptual capacities or from susceptibility to pleasure and pain. We have invented computers to save us the trouble of computing. These machines are not thinking beings who do our thinking for us, but rather devices that produce the results of calculations without *anyone* literally calculating or thinking. What prevents the *literal* application of intellectual concepts to computers is not deficiency of computational power. Rather, it is the fact that it makes no sense to attribute to a machine will or passion, desire or pain. These are capacities of the animate; of beings that have a body – but machines have do not have bodies; of beings that have no intrinsic purpose yet adopt purposes of their own – but machines have whatever intrinsic purpose they are made for and have no purposes of their own; of beings, unlike machines, who set themselves ends, have preferences, likes and dislikes, are pleased to achieve their goals and distressed to fail. They are capacities of beings who have a good, who can flourish or flounder, who have a welfare. But while circumstances may affect the condition of a machine, be good or bad *for it*, they cannot affect the welfare or good of the machine, since it has none. What is inanimate cannot be well or do well. What is lifeless has no welfare.

Thinking is a phenomenon of life. It is exhibited in endlessly varied kinds of behaviour in the stream of life. Its forms are aspects of a form of life, of a culture. We need not fear that our machines will out-think us – though we might well fear that they will lead us to cease to think for ourselves. What they lack is not computational power, but animality. Desire and suffering, hope and frustration are the roots of thought, not mechanical computation.[16]

NOTES

I am grateful to Dr H.-J. Glock, Professor O. Hanfling and Dr J. Hyman for their comments on the first draft of this book.

1. That is, all metaphysical theories concerning the necessary structure of reality, or of the human mind.

2. Hume, *A Treatise of Human Nature* I 1 vi, ed. L.A. Selby-Bigge, 2nd edn revised by P.H. Nidditch (Clarendon Press, Oxford, 1978), p. 252.

3. G. Frege, 'Thoughts', repr. in B. McGuinness (ed.), *Gottlob Frege: Collected Papers on Mathematics, Logic and Philosophy* (Blackwell, Oxford, 1984), p. 360.

4. Ibid., p. 360.

5. Ibid., p. 361.

6. Ibid., p. 367.

7. P.F. Strawson, *Individuals* (Methuen, London, 1959), p. 97f.

8. W. James, *The Principles of Psychology* (1890), (Dover, New York, 1950), Vol. I, p. 185.

9. Thomas Reid, *Essay on the Intellectual Powers of Man*, repr. in Sir William Hamilton (ed.), *The Works of Thomas Reid, D.D.* (Machlachlan and Stewart, Edinburgh, 1863), Vol. I, p. 442.

10. Hume, *A Treatise of Human Nature*, p. 190.

11. James, *The Principles of Psychology*, Vol. I, p. 189f.

12. The quotation 'In the beginning was the deed' is from Goethe's *Faust*.

13. Hume, *A Treatise of Human Nature*, p. 253.

14. J.Z. Young, *Programs of the Brain* (Oxford University Press, Oxford, 1978), p. 119.

15. C. Blakemore, *Mechanics of the Mind* (Cambridge University Press, Cambridge, 1977), p. 91.

16. In this book I have drawn freely on previous writings of mine on Wittgenstein's philosophical psychology. For a much more detailed treatment, see P.M.S. Hacker, *Wittgenstein: Meaning and Mind, Volume 3 of an Analytic Commentary on the Philosophical Investigations*, Part I – The Essays (Blackwell, Oxford, 1993).

ABBREVIATIONS
used to refer to works by Wittgenstein

BB *The Blue and Brown Books* (Blackwell, Oxford, 1958).

BT 'The Big Typescript', excerpts in J. Klagge and A. Nordmann (eds), *Ludwig Wittgenstein: Philosophical Occasions 1912–1951* (Hackett, Indianapolis and Cambridge, 1993), pp. 161–99.

CV *Culture and Value*, ed. G.H. von Wright in collaboration with H. Nyman, tr. P. Winch (Blackwell, Oxford, 1980).

LPE 'Notes for lectures on "Private Experience" and "Sense Data"', ed. R. Rhees, repr. in Klagge and Nordmann, *Ludwig Wittgenstein: Philosophical Occasions 1912–1952*, pp. 202–88.

LSD 'The Language of Sense Data and Private Experience', notes
by R. Rhees, repr. in Klagge and Nordmann, *Ludwig Wittgenstein: Philosophical Occasions 1912–1951*, pp. 290–367.

LW I *Last Writings on the Philosophy of Psychology*, Vol. 1, ed. G.H. von Wright and H. Nyman, tr. C.G. Luckhardt and M.A.E. Aue (Blackwell, Oxford, 1982).

MS 165 Unpublished manuscript number 165.

PI *Philosophical Investigations*, ed. G.E.M. Anscombe and R. Rhees, tr. G.E.M. Anscombe, 2nd edn (Blackwell, Oxford, 1958); references to Part I are by section number (§), to Part II by page.

PR *Philosophical Remarks*, ed. R. Rhees, tr. R. Hargreaves and R. White (Blackwell, Oxford, 1975).

RPP I *Remarks on the Philosophy of Psychology*, Vol. 1, ed. G.E.M. Anscombe and G.H. von Wright, tr. G.E.M. Anscombe (Blackwell, Oxford, 1980).

RPP II *Remarks on the Philosophy of Psychology*, Vol. 2,
ed. G.H. von Wright and H. Nyman, tr. C.G. Luckhardt and
M.A.E. Aue (Blackwell, Oxford, 1980).

Z *Zettel*, ed. G.E.M. Anscombe and G.H. von Wright, tr. G.E.M.
Anscombe (Blackwell, Oxford, 1967).

I have occasionally changed quoted passages where the
translation seemed to me to be unsatisfactory.